Mason Meets Mr. Virus

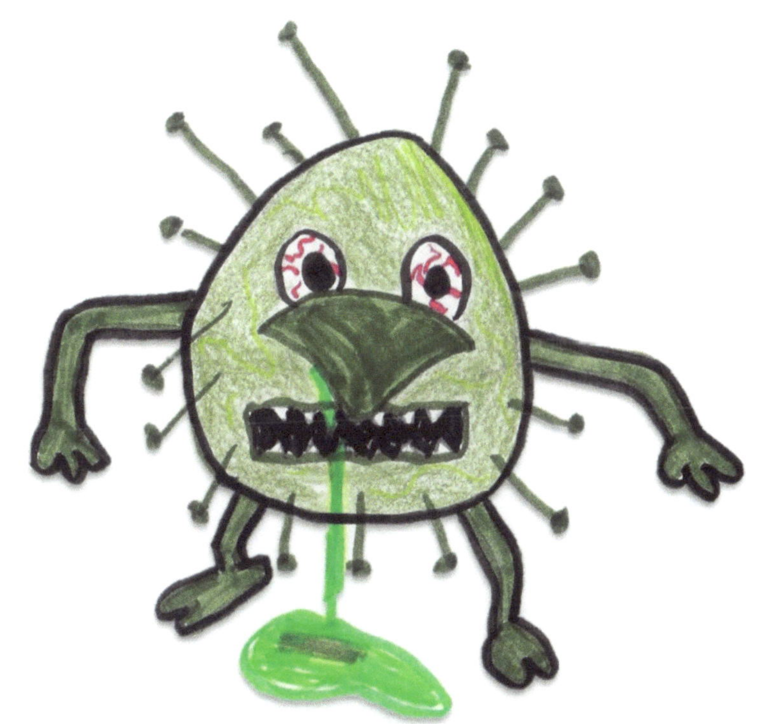

THIS BOOK BELONGS TO:

Jax asked Mason one day.
" What is a Virus?"
"I am not sure Jax but let us
look it up and find out.
It says that a virus is a
submicroscopic infection.
I think they mean a small
bug."

"Come on Billy and Lizzie let us go outside to the back yard to hide from Mr. Virus. He will not find us in the long grass."

Can you find Mason, Billy, and Lizzie?

Jax decided to see if a plane ride
would make Mr. Virus go away.

But After they landed, Mr. Virus was still there!

Mason tried to send Mr. Virus
to the moon.

But Mr. Virus decided to go for a
ride, instead of going to the moon.

Mason put on his knight's costume to fight Mr. Virus

But every time he would go
to strike him with his sword,
Mr. Virus would move away.

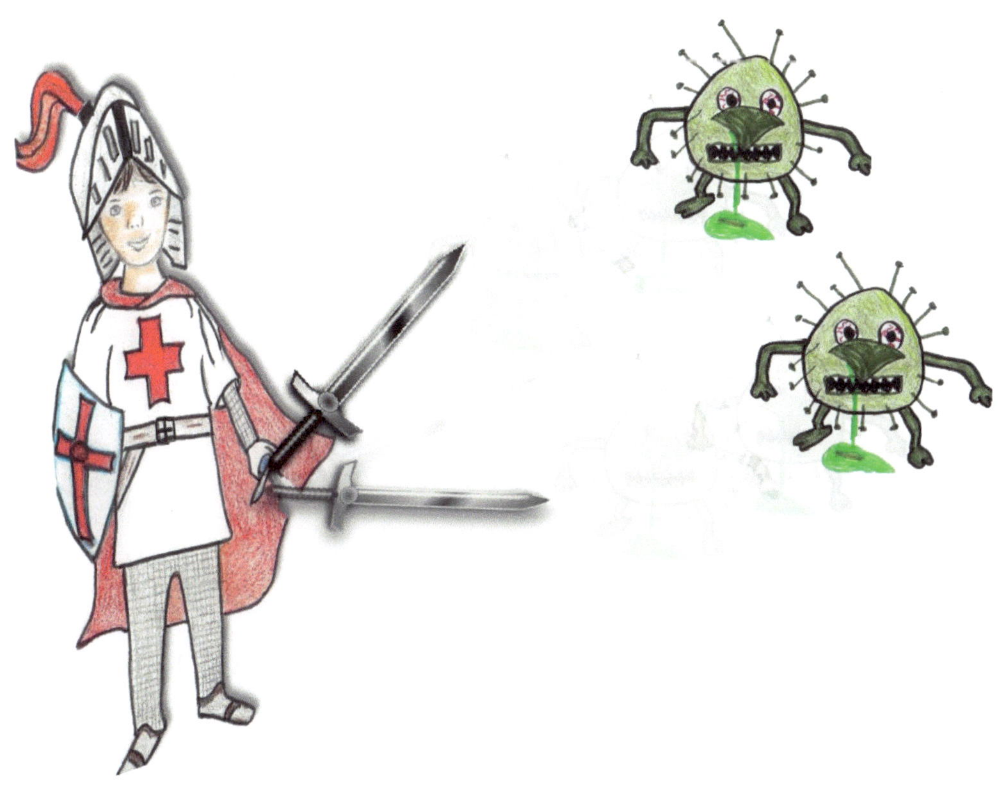

Mason looked in his book for everything
about a virus, and how to get rid of it, and
what to do to stop it from spreading.

He found out that to help stop Mr. Virus from spreading to the ones you love and care about, you should.

Wear a mask

Wash your hands with soap and water

Stay 2 metres apart from the people that do not live in your house.

"Good morning Billy,
look, Mr. Sun is up too!
Let us go downstairs
and see if Mr. Virus is
still here."

"How about
some
breakfast
first, then
we can get
Jax to help
us banish
Mr. Virus."

Mason and Billy started to eat their breakfast when Jax called to them.

"Mason, come look at what they are saying about Mr. Virus on TV. Come see."

"They are saying that Mr. Virus is going on a long trip and with the help of the doctors and scientist we can have a vasa nation so we wont get sick."

Mason thought hard at what Jax just said, and could not understand what he meant. "Jax what is a vasa nation?"

Jax yelled back, "You know when you get a needle in your arm."

Mason laughed, you mean a **<u>Vaccination</u>**."

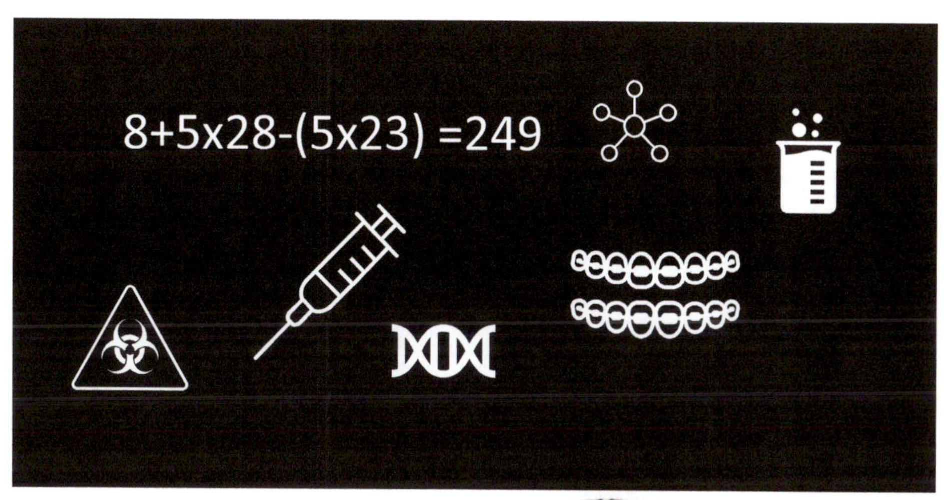

8+5x28-(5x23) =249

Everyone went off to visit the doctor's office. Jax looked at the nurse holding the needle and said. " I think you should go first Mason; I will wait until everyone has had theirs."

Mason looked at his brother and said. "Don't worry Jax, I will go first and show you that I am a Brave Knight, and you can be Spiderman, who fights Viruses and saves the world."
Jax smiled and said, "OK MASON, I will pretend that I have my Spiderman costume on, and you pretend that you have your Knights costume on too."

DOCTOR'S OFFICE

After their visit to the doctors office to get their vaccination, Mason sat down to read his favourite books. I AM A BRAVE KNIGHT, and MASON'S FAMILY IS MOVING. Lizzie sat very quietly while Mason reads to her.
Jax, Hattie and Billy played with their toys while Mommy and Daddy where in the kitchen making dinner.

Mason looked up from his book and said. **"I am sure glad that Mr. Virus has gone away and we do not have to fight him anymore."**

Jax smiled and said, "Yes Mason, me too."